FRANCIS FRITH'S

AROUND CHEAM
INCLUDING SUTTON, EWELL, BANSTEAD AND EPSOM

PHOTOGRAPHIC MEMORIES

KEITH HOWELL, writer and broadcaster, is a member of the British Guild of Travel Writers and a Liveryman of the Worshipful Company of Musicians. He was born and brought up in Surrey, was educated at Epsom, and has spent much of his life living and working in Surrey, where he still resides.

FRANCIS FRITH'S
PHOTOGRAPHIC MEMORIES

AROUND CHEAM
INCLUDING SUTTON, EWELL, BANSTEAD AND EPSOM

PHOTOGRAPHIC MEMORIES

KEITH HOWELL

First published in the United Kingdom in 2005
by The Francis Frith Collection

Hardback edition published in 2005 ISBN 1-84589-009-4

Paperback edition published in 2005 ISBN 1-85937-467-0

Text and Design copyright The Francis Frith Collection®
Photographs copyright The Francis Frith Collection®
except where indicated.

The Frith® photographs and the Frith® logo are reproduced under
licence from Heritage Photographic Resources Ltd, the owners of the
Frith® archive and trademarks.
'The Francis Frith Collection', 'Francis Frith' and 'Frith' are
registered trademarks of Heritage Photographic Resources Ltd.

All rights reserved. No photograph in this publication may be sold
to a third party other than in the original form of this publication,
or framed for sale to a third party. No parts of this publication
may be reproduced, stored in a retrieval system, or transmitted, in
any form, or by any means, electronic, mechanical, photocopying,
recording or otherwise, without the prior permission of the
publishers and copyright holder.

British Library Cataloguing in Publication Data

Around Cheam, including Sutton, Ewell,
Banstead and Epsom - Photographic Memories
Keith Howell

The Francis Frith Collection
Frith's Barn, Teffont,
Salisbury, Wiltshire SP3 5QP
Tel: +44 (0) 1722 716 376
Email: info@francisfrith.co.uk
www.francisfrith.co.uk

Printed and bound in Great Britain

Front Cover: **CHEAM**, *The Broadway 1932* 85087t
Frontispiece: **EPSOM**, *Ruxley Splash 1907* 58600

*The colour-tinting is for illustrative purposes only, and is not intended
to be historically accurate*

Aerial photographs reproduced under licence from
Simmons Aerofilms Limited.
Historical Ordnance Survey maps reproduced under licence from
Homecheck.co.uk

Every attempt has been made to contact copyright holders of
illustrative material. We will be happy to give full acknowledgement
in future editions for any items not credited. Any information
should be directed to The Francis Frith Collection.

AS WITH ANY HISTORICAL DATABASE THE FRITH ARCHIVE IS
CONSTANTLY BEING CORRECTED AND IMPROVED AND THE
PUBLISHERS WOULD WELCOME INFORMATION ON OMISSIONS OR
INACCURACIES

CONTENTS

FRANCIS FRITH: VICTORIAN PIONEER	7
AROUND CHEAM - AN INTRODUCTION	10
CHEAM FROM THE AIR	14
SUTTON AND NORTH CHEAM	16
ORDNANCE SURVEY MAP OF CHEAM	26
CHEAM: THE VILLAGE	28
FROM CHEAM TO EWELL AND EPSOM	44
COUNTY MAP	70
CHEAM IN THE FIFTIES	72
CHEAM TO THE SOUTH	84
INDEX	89
NAMES OF SUBSCRIBERS	90
Free Mounted Print Voucher	93

FRANCIS FRITH
VICTORIAN PIONEER

FRANCIS FRITH, founder of the world-famous photographic archive, was a complex and multi-talented man. A devout Quaker and a highly successful Victorian businessman, he was philosophical by nature and pioneering in outlook.

By 1855 he had already established a wholesale grocery business in Liverpool, and sold it for the astonishing sum of £200,000, which is the equivalent today of over £15,000,000. Now a very rich man, he was able to indulge his passion for travel. As a child he had pored over travel books written by early explorers, and his fancy and imagination had been stirred by family holidays to the sublime mountain regions of Wales and Scotland. 'What lands of spirit-stirring and enriching scenes and places!' he had written. He was to return to these scenes of grandeur in later years to 'recapture the thousands of vivid and tender memories', but with a different purpose. Now in his thirties, and captivated by the new science of photography, Frith set out on a series of pioneering journeys up the Nile and to the Near East that occupied him from 1856 until 1860.

INTRIGUE AND EXPLORATION

These far-flung journeys were packed with intrigue and adventure. In his life story, written when he was sixty-three, Frith tells of being held captive by bandits, and of fighting 'an awful midnight battle to the very point of surrender with a deadly pack of hungry, wild dogs'. Wearing flowing Arab costume, Frith arrived at Akaba by camel sixty years before Lawrence of Arabia, where he encountered 'desert princes and rival sheikhs, blazing with jewel-hilted swords'.

He was the first photographer to venture beyond the sixth cataract of the Nile. Africa was still the mysterious 'Dark Continent', and Stanley and Livingstone's historic meeting was a decade into the future. The conditions for picture taking confound belief. He laboured for hours in his wicker dark-room in the sweltering heat of the desert, while the volatile chemicals fizzed dangerously in their trays. Back in London he exhibited his photographs and was 'rapturously cheered' by members of the Royal Society. His reputation as a photographer was made overnight.

VENTURE OF A LIFE-TIME

Characteristically, Frith quickly spotted the opportunity to create a new business as a specialist publisher of photographs. He lived in an era of immense and sometimes violent change.

For the poor in the early part of Victoria's reign work was exhausting and the hours long, and people had precious little free time to enjoy themselves. Most had no transport other than a cart or gig at their disposal, and rarely travelled far beyond the boundaries of their own town or village. However, by the 1870s the railways had threaded their way across the country, and Bank Holidays and half-day Saturdays had been made obligatory by Act of Parliament. All of a sudden the working man and his family were able to enjoy days out and see a little more of the world.

With typical business acumen, Francis Frith foresaw that these new tourists would enjoy having souvenirs to commemorate their days out. In 1860 he married Mary Ann Rosling and set out on a new career: his aim was to photograph every city, town and village in Britain. For the next thirty years he travelled the country by train and by pony and trap, producing fine photographs of seaside resorts and beauty spots that were keenly bought by millions of Victorians. These prints were painstakingly pasted into family albums and pored over during the dark nights of winter, rekindling precious memories of summer excursions.

THE RISE OF FRITH & CO

Frith's studio was soon supplying retail shops all over the country. To meet the demand he gathered about him a small team of photographers, and published the work of independent artist-photographers of the calibre of Roger Fenton and Francis Bedford. In order to gain some understanding of the scale of Frith's business one only has to look at the catalogue issued by Frith & Co in 1886: it runs to some 670 pages, listing not only many thousands of views of the British Isles but also many photographs of most European countries, and China, Japan, the USA and Canada - note the sample page shown on page 9 from the hand-written Frith & Co ledgers recording the pictures. By 1890 Frith had created the greatest specialist photographic publishing company in the world, with over 2,000 sales outlets - more than the combined number that Boots and WH Smith have today! The picture on the next page shows the Frith & Co display board at Ingleton in the Yorkshire Dales (left of window). Beautifully constructed with a mahogany frame and gilt inserts, it could display up to a dozen local scenes.

POSTCARD BONANZA

The ever-popular holiday postcard we know today took many years to develop. In 1870 the Post Office issued the first plain cards, with a pre-printed stamp on one face. In 1894 they allowed other publishers' cards to be sent through the mail with an attached adhesive halfpenny stamp. Demand grew rapidly, and in 1895 a new size of postcard was permitted called the court card, but there was little room for illustration. In 1899, a year after Frith's death, a new card measuring 5.5 x 3.5 inches became the standard format, but it was not until 1902 that the divided back came into being, so that the address and message could be on one face and a full-size illustration on the other. Frith & Co were in the vanguard of postcard development: Frith's sons Eustace and Cyril continued their father's monumental task, expanding the number of views offered to the public and recording more and more places in Britain, as the coasts and countryside were opened up to mass travel.

Francis Frith had died in 1898 at his villa in Cannes, his great project still growing. The archive he created continued in business for another seventy years. By 1970 it contained over a third of a million pictures showing 7,000 British towns and villages.

FRANCIS FRITH'S LEGACY

Frith's legacy to us today is of immense significance and value, for the magnificent archive of evocative photographs he created provides a unique record of change in the cities, towns and villages throughout Britain over a century and more. Frith and his fellow studio photographers revisited locations many times down the years to update their views, compiling for us an enthralling and colourful pageant of British life and character.

We are fortunate that Frith was dedicated to recording the minutiae of everyday life, for it is this sheer wealth of visual data, the painstaking chronicle of changes in dress, transport, street layouts, buildings, housing, engineering and landscape that captivates us so much today. His remarkable images offer us a powerful link with the past and with the lives of our ancestors.

THE VALUE OF THE ARCHIVE TODAY

Computers have now made it possible for Frith's many thousands of images to be accessed almost instantly. Frith's images are increasingly used as visual resources, by social historians, by researchers into genealogy and ancestry, by architects and town planners, and by teachers involved in local history projects.

In addition, the archive offers every one of us an opportunity to examine the places where we and our families have lived and worked down the years. Highly successful in Frith's own era, the archive is now, a century and more on, entering a new phase of popularity. Historians consider the Francis Frith Collection to be of prime national importance. It is the only archive of its kind remaining in private ownership. Francis Frith's archive is now housed in an historic timber barn in the beautiful village of Teffont in Wiltshire. Its founder would not recognize the archive office as it is today. In place of the many thousands of dusty boxes containing glass plate negatives and an all-pervading odour of photographic chemicals, there are now ranks of computer screens. He would be amazed to watch his images travelling round the world at unimaginable speeds through internet lines.

The archive's future is both bright and exciting. Francis Frith, with his unshakeable belief in making photographs available to the greatest number of people, would undoubtedly approve of what is being done today with his lifetime's work. His photographs depicting our shared past are now bringing pleasure and enlightenment to millions around the world a century and more after his death.

AROUND CHEAM
AN INTRODUCTION

'A rather small and commonplace village on the Epsom road, a short distance from Carshalton. Rents rather high'.
Dickens's 'Dictionary of London' 1879

'It was like Beverley Hills to me. I thought it was the poshest place I'd ever seen'.
Ray Galton

THE ORIGINAL human settlement of Cheam dates back at least a thousand years: the remains of hut circles were still visible until recently on Banstead Downs, and examples of early British and Roman coins and pottery were discovered in the area during the opening decades of the last century. Inevitably, it was the presence of water which encouraged these early settlers to establish themselves here on the reverse slope of the North Downs, where the huge chalk mass is briefly covered by a narrow bed of Thanet sand extending from Croydon to Epsom, before

CHEAM, *Haymaking in Nonsuch Park 1925* 77074

London clay comes to predominate as one approaches the River Thames. These clay soils of the Thames Valley provided mainly only poor-quality surface water, but on the sandy soils excellent water could be obtained from wells along the spring line.

During the Saxon settlement of England, the entire country was divided into parishes, which were usually laid out in squares with the church, manor-house and village houses in a central position, surrounded by cultivated fields, and with common pastureland around the outside. But because of the clustering of settlements along this spring line, the arrangement was adjusted so that these parishes covered an area of roughly three miles in length by three-quarters of a mile in width, to form a series of long, narrow administrative areas.

In old documents, Cheam has been spelt in around fourteen different ways, including Cheiham, Kaham, Keyham and Cheiham, and in the Domesday survey as Ceiham. Before 1018, Cheam had belonged to the under-kings and was held by the Abbot and Convent of Chertsey, but it was then given by the Saxon king Athelstan to the monks of Christ Church, Canterbury – they issued the warning that anyone who infringed their rights would be 'excommincatus cum diablo societur'. After the Conquest, Archbishop Lanfranc divided Cheam into two manors, East and West Cheam, keeping the former himself and allotting the other to the monks. It is believed that about the time of the Domesday survey, there were around three hundred inhabitants and some fifty houses.

In 1539, Archbishop Cranmer exchanged the manor of East Cheam with Henry VIII for Chislet Park in Kent, and on the dissolution of the monasteries Henry also took possession of West Cheam manor. In 1537, he purchased the village, church and estate of neighbouring Cuddington parish from Sir Richard Codington and, having demolished the buildings there, embarked on his plan to build the magnificent Palace of Nonsuch using a Florentine architect. It was still only half finished at the time of his death in 1547. Even so, both he and his female successor Queen Elizabeth I spent much time here.

Cheam acquired great importance from its proximity to the Palace of Nonsuch, and it was an association that was to continue beyond Elizabeth's reign, for it was visited by James I and Charles I. The plague which swept London in 1665 appears to have left the inhabitants of Cheam unscathed, although it saw the transfer of a school from the capital which was to remain here until 1934, and which was to number the second Queen Elizabeth's consort amongst its pupils.

Even so, along with the neighbouring finger parishes of Beddington, Carshalton, Sutton, Ewell and Epsom, Cheam remained largely untouched by its proximity to the capital to the north, and it was not until the coming of the railways in the early decades of the Victorian era that changes began to take place in what was essentially a rural economy.

Cheam Station, on the Victoria line, opened in 1847, and in the initial years freight formed the principal business of the railway, along with intermittent race traffic to Epsom. In 1801 the population of Cheam numbered 616 people, and fifty years later had only just doubled. But by the turn of that century Cheam had nearly three and a half thousand inhabitants, with neighbouring Sutton having more than seventeen thousand, owing largely to its role as a major coaching centre on the main Brighton road.

And it was in the opening decades of the 20th century that both Cheam and Sutton witnessed their most spectacular expansion. Improved railway connections to London, and the desirability of life away from the noise and foul atmosphere of the rapidly expanding conurbation, had made this district a prime target for developers and new residents. Unlike Sutton, however, the opportunities for Cheam's development had been limited by the village being hemmed in by Cheam Park on the west and by Cheam Manor on the east, and no houses could be built on the chalk downs because of the inaccessibility of water supplies. But in the early 1860s, the Sutton Water Company was incorporated, and mains were laid along the Brighton road, the Carshalton road, and shortly afterwards to Cheam, making much of the chalk and London clay land available for building.

Up until the early 1920s Cheam, by virtue of its limited opportunities for development, had still retained the appearance and feel of a small country village. But then the Cheam House estate, Cheam Court Farm, and the old brewery at the crossroads came onto the market and were all demolished, leading to the creation of much of the village centre as it is today. Southwards, large detached suburban houses occupied much of what had once been open downland, while the opening of the Sutton bypass in 1927 and the widening of the east-west road linking Croydon and Epsom both encouraged the growth of motor traffic through the area.

By the start of the Second World War, much of the centre of the village had been redeveloped to cater for an ever-growing population, while still managing to keep much of its appealing character. But it was in the 1950s that the name of Cheam came to national, if not international, prominence. In November 1954, scriptwriters Ray Galton and Alan Simpson first launched their immortal comic creation 'Hancock's Half

EWELL, *High Street 1924* 75489

Hour' on BBC Radio. Featuring its eponymous and bombastic hero Anthony Aloysius St John Hancock and assorted companions, it was set at what has become one of the best-known of all fictional addresses: 23 Railway Cuttings, East Cheam. Over the course of thirty-six episodes of the now venerated radio and television shows, the events at Hancock's mythical residence entertained audiences until December 1959.

So how did Cheam come to figure so enduringly in this classic comedy, to the point where for years anyone living in the area inevitably found themselves being greeted with a broad smile whenever they mentioned their own address? Recently, Ray Galton told me how it dated back to his own childhood years:

'Although I was born in Paddington, my parents and I moved to the Rosehill estate at St. Helier, and during the war years, when I was around nine or ten, I used to catch the bus to Cheam on Saturday mornings to earn half-a-crown pocket money helping a milkman on his round from the United Dairies depot in the Ewell Road. It was with a horse and cart, and, incidentally, the horse was a real character. He refused to go out with any other driver, and he knew exactly when we were about to make the final delivery on the round. As soon as we'd made the last stop, he'd gallop off back down Sandy Lane and Burdon Lane to the depot with me hanging on to the back trying to stop the crates of empty bottles flying off all over the road. Anyway, Cheam was like Beverley Hills to me. I thought it was the poshest place I'd ever seen. So when we came to write 'Hancock's Half Hour', we wanted a place for Hancock which fitted in with his lofty aspirations to be a part of smart society, but one which, of course, didn't quite make it and was on the fringes. So we settled on East Cheam.'

While East Cheam manor house in Gander Green Lane had been demolished long ago, and well before Ray and his quirky equine companion began clinking their way around the middle-class mansions south of the village, Hancock's address had more than a hint of historical basis in fact. When the branch line from Sutton to Wimbledon was constructed in 1928, it had necessitated the excavation of a substantial amount of soil to create the cutting that carries the line to West Sutton Station, which was then added to the grounds of Sutton Cricket Club. So, in theory, Hancock's legendary residence should have been positioned somewhere in the vicinity of Western Road. Perhaps Messrs Galton and Simpson unwittingly came perilously close to giving their fictional creation a real address.

Henry VIII and his daughter Elizabeth no longer chase the deer in Nonsuch and Cuddington; the milk floats have vanished from the United Dairies depot; no faint strains of traditional jazz echo from the assembly room of the Queen Victoria; and there is no ice cream on sale in what was once the foyer of the Century cinema. But those of us who remember Cheam as it is captured in these pictures will be thankful that so much of its charm is still preserved today.

FRANCIS FRITH'S - AROUND CHEAM

CHEAM FROM THE AIR

CHEAM *from the air 1964* AFA130110

SUTTON AND NORTH CHEAM

SUTTON, *Gander Green Lane 1898* 41716
This road formed the old parish boundary between Sutton and Cheam. At its southern extremity and the junction with Cheam Road was the site of East Cheam Manor and a dozen or so houses. This view, looking north, shows the small roadside pond in the middle distance which existed on the east side of the road, midway between the S-bend and what is now West Sutton railway station. On the left are the grounds of the Lower Cheam House estate.

SUTTON AND NORTH CHEAM

SUTTON
High Street c1960 S233056

At this major junction of Cheam Road, Carshalton Road and the steep High Street, the splendid and ornate sign of the Cock Hotel with the Courage Brewery rooster mounted above sits in the centre. On the right is the three-storey shop of the bookseller and stationer's William Pile, whose interior exuded the rich aroma of leather bindings. Next door are the offices and showrooms of the South Eastern Electricity Board. Further down the hill, on the corner of Throwley Road, the cupola surmounting the Municipal Offices rises above the surrounding buildings. Beyond is the white stone frontage of the Gaumont Cinema.

SUTTON, *High Street c1965* S233103
This marvellously detailed view of the High Street before it was transformed into a pedestrian precinct was taken from the first floor of the Cock Hotel. On the left, next to the Lloyd's Bank branch, is the fashion shop of Renee Shaw, with Fuller's tea shop, Dewhurst's the butcher's, and John's menswear shop further down the hill. Shinner's large department store with its clock over the pavement is visible (centre left), and so is the white frontage of Perring's furniture showroom on the corner of West Street. On the right, William Pile's premises have been absorbed into the showrooms of Seeboard.

SUTTON
Cheam Road c1955
S233005

Strangely devoid of motor traffic, this view of the Cheam Road captures a small group of adults and schoolboys waiting at the bus stop on the right for a 213, 408 or 470 bus to transport them westwards to Cheam or Epsom. The Cock Hotel across the traffic lights has the police station and the Congregational Church beyond, while on the adjacent corner William Pile's shop has a window display of books, calendars and cards. On the extreme left is the forecourt of the Curzon cinema, with Ann Laurie's confectionery shop and Symington & Stedman's estate agency heading the parade of small shops closer to the crossroads.

SUTTON
Cheam Road c1955
S233031

The convergent flying buttresses of the 1907 Trinity Methodist Church spire soar above the mock-Tudor frontages over the parade of shops at the start of Cheam Road, with the Edwardian cupola of the Curzon Cinema immediately below. On the right the branch of Teekoff Ltd, with its coffee-roasting machine prominent in the near window, would entice customers from the bus stop on the opposite pavement with its fragrant aromas.

SUTTON AND NORTH CHEAM

▲ **SUTTON,** *Cheam Road c1961* S233083

The Curzon Cinema, on the left, opened its doors for business in 1911 as the Cheam Road Cinema. Although much smaller in capacity than the two nearby picture houses, the Granada and the Gaumont, it managed to survive into the 1970s, when its stylish façade was removed and it was transformed into a nightclub called Legends. At the time this picture was taken it was showing 'The Parent Trap' starring Hayley Mills and Maureen O'Hara.

◄ **SUTTON**
Cheam Road c1960
S233092

The raised pavements on both sides of Cheam Road at this point are lined with substantial trees. Between those on the right is the south porch of Trinity Methodist Church. Just beyond, a saloon car turns into Church Road, at the foot of which stands the parish church of St Nicholas. As a result of the development of Sutton, this is now St Nicholas Way. In the distance a single-decker bus, probably a 213 from Kingston and Cheam, approaches the crossroads at the Cock Hotel.

NORTH CHEAM
The Queen Victoria c1960 N258063

The original inn, which stood on the site of the London Road tollgate, was replaced in 1936 by this impressive roadhouse with its large forecourt and function rooms. In the 1950s one of the latter was the weekly venue for the North Cheam Jazz Club, which featured a youthful George Melly and the Mick Mulligan Jazz Band as a regular attraction. This building was demolished in 1964 when the site was redeveloped.

NORTH CHEAM
Malden Road and London Road c1960
C70074

The immaculately maintained flowerbeds and lawn outside the Queen Victoria have provided one passer-by with an opportunity to rest and watch the passing traffic at this busy junction. Across the Malden road, the parade of shops with flats above date from the mid 1930s.

FRANCIS FRITH'S - AROUND CHEAM

SUTTON AND NORTH CHEAM

NORTH CHEAM
London Road c1955
N258045

Here we have another view of this heavily traffic-ridden main road with its shopping parade. On the right, Raymond's hair salon proudly advertises its offer of 'perms from fifteen shillings'. Although this equates to 75 pence in today's currency, it would have represented a substantial outlay for most women in the 1950s. At the far end of the parade is the prominent sign for the Granada cinema, which had opened in October 1937 showing the Fred Astaire and Ginger Rogers musical film 'Shall We Dance?'. The cinema seated two thousand people, had a Wurlitzer organ, and boasted that its patrons would breathe air which had been 'laundered in a synthetic mountain stream'.

FRANCIS FRITH'S - AROUND CHEAM

▶ **NORTH CHEAM**
*London Road
c1955* N258039

The broad expanse of the A24 London Road heading towards Stonecot Hill and Morden is lined with parked cars and bicycles outside the shops. On the extreme right is the local branch of the shoe chain Freeman Hardy & Willis, with F W Woolworths next door.

◀ **SUTTON**
*The Woodstock,
Stonecot Hill c1955*
S233051

The Woodstock, constructed in the 1930s, continues to flourish today as it clearly did when this photograph was taken with these cars parked in the forecourt, although the frontage of the pub has since been painted and one of the brick gate piers at the entrance removed.

SUTTON AND NORTH CHEAM

▲ **SUTTON,** *Stonecot Hill c1955* S233047

The line of concrete lamp standards, surmounted by the new sodium streetlights, delineates the edges of the A24 as it ascends from its crossing over the Pyl brook towards Morden. In the background on the right is the bulk of the red brick St Anthony's Hospital, designed by James Emes, which was opened at the beginning of the First World War and whose beds were soon occupied by sick and wounded soldiers. This building was demolished in 1978, and was succeeded by the present complex.

◀ **CHEAM**
The Gander Inn c1955
C70027

At the foot of St Dunstan's Hill, this mock-Tudor fronted Charrington's pub stands at the crossing point of the old parish boundary of Gander Green Lane with the Sutton by-pass, which had been constructed in 1927 on the A217, and carried Brighton-bound traffic away from Sutton's developing centre, skirting Cheam village centre in the process.

FRANCIS FRITH'S - AROUND CHEAM

SUTTON AND NORTH CHEAM

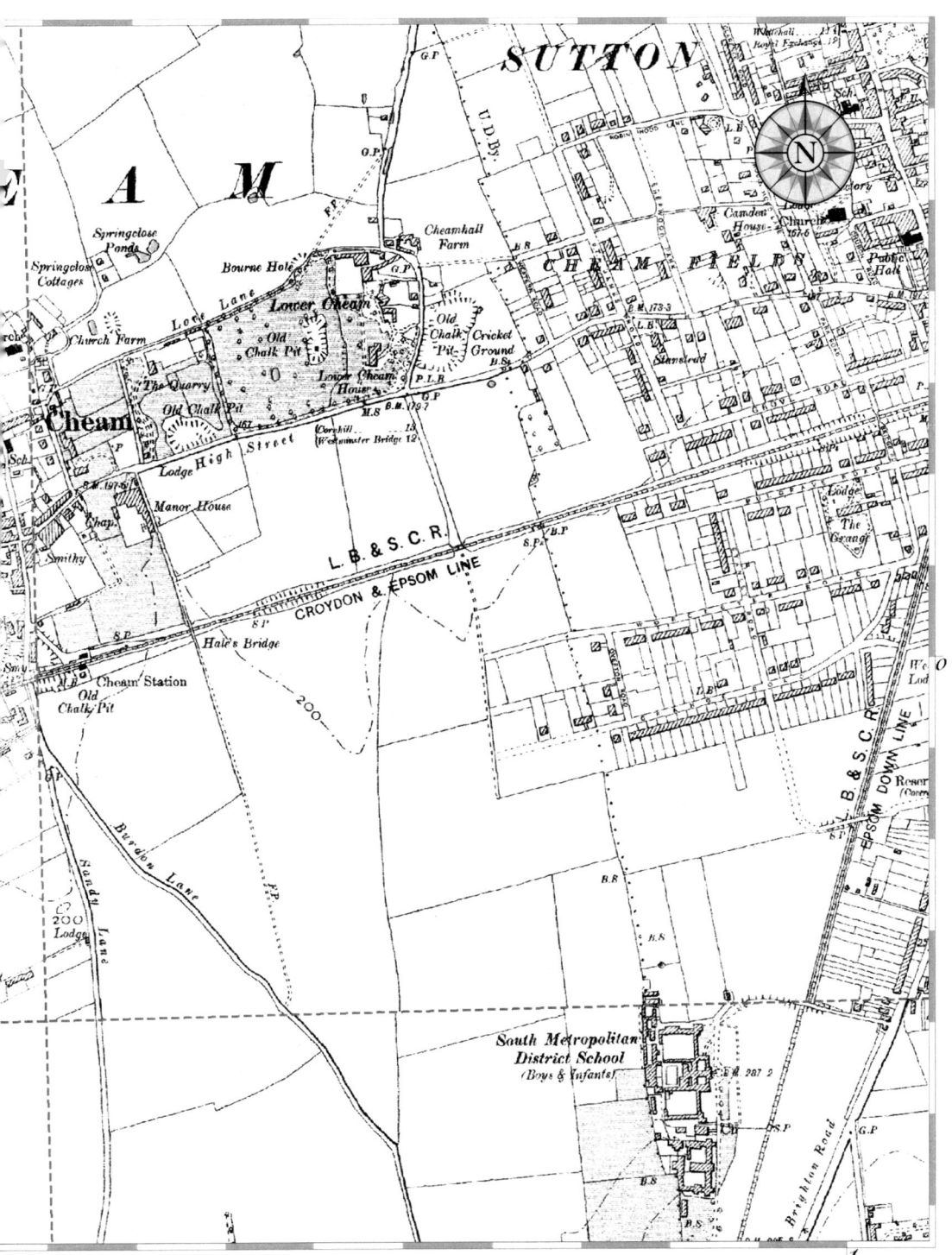

ORDNANCE SURVEY MAP OF CHEAM AND SURROUNDING AREAS c1850

CHEAM: THE VILLAGE

CHEAM, *Malden Road 1894* 34067

There are still many reminders of this view visible today if one looks north from the entrance to the war memorial gardens. The builder and undertaker's shop on the extreme right was on the corner of Church Road, and the frontage of the adjacent cottage is little altered. Further along the road are the King's Hall, advertising 'teas and dances', and the Prince of Wales public house. On the left the Scout Hall (now St Dunstan's Institute) remains, but an entrance to Mickleham Gardens bisects the rectory wall.

CHEAM: THE VILLAGE

CHEAM
*The School Chapel
1904* 51200

Built in 1867, this ivy-festooned building was considered to be one of the finest private chapels in the county. When the school moved to Berkshire in 1934, the owners considered the idea of taking it with them, but the costs and problems of dismantling, transporting and re-erecting the building were eventually recognised as impractical. It remains in Dallas Road today as St Christopher's Roman Catholic Church.

CHEAM, *The School 1904* 51199

The school, initially installed at Whitehall on Malden Road in the year of the Great Plague of 1665, moved to this site (now occupied by Tabor Court alongside the present by-pass) in 1719. This photograph shows the playground at the rear of the school buildings. The fourth storey and the extensions were added in the 1860s. The leafless tree is a venerable false acacia, which was a feature of the playground for many years, while the tree on the left still stands in the garage yard of Tabor Court.

FRANCIS FRITH'S - AROUND CHEAM

▲ **CHEAM**
High Street 1925 77051

This peaceful view of the old High Street looks down the hill to the Harrow Inn at the bottom. The house on the right was Vine Cottage, where Mr Dealy, the butler at Cheam School, lived with his family. The milk churn partially protected from the sun on its 'pram', which bears the initials WWS on its tailgate, is from Winslow Sergeant's Dairy at Pond Hill farm. His son opened the cycle shop in Malden Road in 1921on his return from service in the First World War.

▶ *detail from* 77051

CHEAM: THE VILLAGE

CHEAM
Park Lane 1925 77055

The timber framed jettied house called Whitehall, standing on the corner of Park Lane and Malden Road, is thought to have been built as a farmhouse c1500, and over the last five centuries it has undergone numerous alterations and additions. At the time this photograph was taken it was still a private residence, but it was subsequently acquired and restored by the local borough council in 1963, and is now opened regularly to the public.

CHEAM, *Whitehall 1925* 77064

Here we have another view of Whitehall, and the adjoining properties of Laurel Cottage and Vault Cottage along the Malden Road, with the elegant rectory beyond which, in its earliest parts, dates back to 1575. According to tradition, an undercroft existed behind these cottages where the first pupils of Cheam School assembled to escape the ravages of the plague of London in 1665. The area was covered in during the 1930s.

CHEAM
Park Lane 1925 77062

These picturesque and simple weatherboarded cottages were once among many in the old village; they were originally built for workers on the Nonsuch estate. In the centre two women, one holding a baby in her arms, watch the photographer at work.

CHEAM: THE VILLAGE

◀ **CHEAM**
Cheam Park House Lodge 1938 88279

This building at the foot of Park Lane, with its stuccoed walls, pedimented porch, and ornamental iron gates, was built around 1820 as the lodge to Cheam Park House. That edifice failed to survive the Second World War, having been wrecked by a V1 flying bomb in July 1944. Its owners then gave the park to the borough council. The lodge, in Park Lane, is still standing, although in a sadly dilapidated condition.

◀ **CHEAM,** *Park Road 1925* 77063

The façade of Ye Olde Red Lion pub in Park Road had undergone some minor changes shortly before this photograph was taken, with the removal of two decorative signboards above the main doorway and the replacement of a Victorian lamp above the entrance with the glass globe. One of the signboards advertised the wares of the Mitcham & Cheam Brewery Company, whose local brewery was situated at the main crossroads of the village. The lettering on the windows closest to the camera advertises teas and dinners, while that on the far window lists brandies, wines and whiskies. In the distance Whitehall, on the Malden Road, is visible.

CHEAM: THE VILLAGE

CHEAM
St Dunstan's Church and the Lychgate 1925
77068

The broach spire of the church with its lancet windows and its tower were added to the original structure in 1870. Its position on a low hill, along with the needle spire, makes it a very prominent landmark for miles around, particularly when the structure is floodlit for special occasions. The function of the lychgate was to provide shelter for pallbearers awaiting the arrival of a funeral cortege. The wall on the extreme right of the photograph once marked the boundary of West Cheam Manor.

◀ **CHEAM**
*St Dunstan's Church
1890* 27584

The church of St Dunstan, relatively new at the time of this photograph, had been built in 1862-64 by G A Pownall in florid French Gothic style alongside the old medieval church, which was largely demolished after the new building was completed. Only the east window and chancel were preserved as the Lumley Chapel, which can be seen on the right of the picture behind the small fir tree.

CHEAM: THE VILLAGE

◀ **CHEAM**
*The Lumley Chapel, the Interior
1890* 27586

This photograph shows some of the numerous monuments housed within the Lumley Chapel that once formed part of old Cheam Church. The carved alabaster tomb of the first Lady Lumley, who died in 1592, dominates this view of the chapel's south side. She was the daughter of Henry Fitzalan, the eighteenth Earl of Arundel, and is depicted on the panel above the tomb's marble top kneeling at prayer. The two front panels show her three children, with the family's coat of arms emblazoned on the damaged end panel. On the extreme left is the carved memorial to James Bovey and his wife. He was probably connected to Cheam School and died in 1695.

◀ **CHEAM,** *St Dunstan's Church 1932* 84917

The brick and ornamented stone interior of the church was augmented by the chancel screen, installed here in 1931, which was designed by Ryan Tenison and had formerly stood in the chapel of St John's College, Battersea. When that chapel was demolished, the screen was presented to St Dunstan's rector, the Rev Canon Wesley Dennis, who had previously been the principal of the college. At the same time the chancel walls were panelled, new altar rails were installed, and a new pulpit was erected.

▲ **CHEAM**
The Old Cottage 1925 77066

This timber-framed Tudor cottage originally occupied a site in Malden Road (now the Broadway) closer to the main crossroads, but it stood in the way of the eventual widening of the street. In 1922, it was completely dismantled and re-erected further north; however, it is regrettable that its original 'rye dough' infilling (clay mixed with rye straw) was replaced with Portland cement. It has more recently succumbed to the demands of Mammon – it is now a bridal shop.

CHEAM: THE VILLAGE

◄ **CHEAM**
The Broadway
1932 85087

We can just see the old cottage of photograph 77066 again in its new location, on the left and partially concealed by the leafy tree. Next to it is the large building occupied for many years by Messrs Sainsbury's Cheam branch. The number of privately owned motor vehicles in the picture demonstrates why the widening of the roadway became necessary during the rapid development of the village in the 1920s and 30s.

◄ **CHEAM,** *Ewell Road 1925* 77054

An open-topped bus trundles along the Ewell Road towards the crossroads of the village, passing the petrol pump of the small garage near the entrance to Park Lane, and with the trees on the edge of Nonsuch Park in the background. The newly constructed offices of the estate agents Soar & Soar flank one side of the Lloyd's Bank branch, whilst behind the rear of the Hamptons furniture van on the right of the picture is the upper floor of the United Dairies premises. The Cheam Brewery had previously occupied this site from the 12th century, and its cellars lie underneath the triangular grassed areas marked by white posts with linking chains.

CHEAM: THE VILLAGE

CHEAM
Ewell Road 1932 85088

A lone policeman in his high-buttoned tunic directs traffic emerging from the Ewell Road to cross the junction with Station Way, The Broadway and the High Street. On the left of the picture is the new building housing the local branches of the stationers and newsagents W H Smith & Son (still there today), Boots the Chemists and Teekoff, the tea and coffee merchants, with flats above; it occupied the site where Cheam Court Farmhouse had stood until the end of the previous decade.

FRANCIS FRITH'S - AROUND CHEAM

CHEAM
Ewell Road 1927 79469

Two cars enter the Ewell Road from the main village crossroads watched by a policeman on point duty at the foot of Station Road (later renamed Station Way). The creeper-covered house on the right is Cheam Court Farmhouse. Behind the police officer is the Plough Inn, which belonged to Cheam Brewery, and was demolished in 1935 along with an adjoining draper's shop run by W D Harris. Above the third vehicle, making its way down the High Street towards the junction, is the sign of the original Harrow Inn, which was demolished in 1934 and replaced

CHEAM, *Ewell Road 1934* 86078
A lady walks briskly across Station Way towards Cheam Court and the local branch of Teekoff, which had a sister establishment in the Cheam Road at Sutton. Beyond, and on the same side of Ewell Road, two suspended lanterns mark the premises of a branch of the Home & Colonial grocery chain. A branch of the Co-operative Stores faces its competitor from across the road, next to the shop with its awning lowered. The car in the middle of the road is turning into the forecourt of Cheam Motors, whose impressive new showrooms are surmounted by a large clock.

CHEAM: THE VILLAGE

CHEAM
The Broadway 1938
88276

This view was taken looking north along the Broadway from the crossroads, showing the extent of the redevelopment carried out by the Onyx Property Investment Company over the two preceding decades and which, while witnessing the demolition of many of the old original buildings, tastefully attempted to capture the Tudor style in its modern architecture.

CHEAM, *Station Way 1938* 88278

The popular Century Cinema was built in 1937 on the corner of Kingsway Road and Station Way. As an independent operation it did not have access to the jealously guarded right to exhibit films for the first time, and flourished on a regimen of re-runs and foreign films. 'The Scarlet Pimpernel', for example, starring Leslie Howard, Merle Oberon and Raymond Massey, had initially been released to the major cinema chains in 1935. Nevertheless, the Century survived until 1960, when it finally closed for business. But the main auditorium was not pulled down for another thirty years, when the whole site was redeveloped.

FROM CHEAM TO EWELL AND EPSOM

NONSUCH PARK, *Bellgate Entrance 1925* 77073

This is the eastern entrance to Nonsuch Park, with the stone cross and drinking fountain erected in 1895 to the memory of W F Gamul Farmer by his eleven surviving children. He and his large family had occupied Cheam Park House in the Victorian era. The memorial was later moved a few feet to accommodate traffic safety requirements, but the brick piers of the gateway with their wrought-iron gates are all still in situ.

FROM CHEAM TO EWELL AND EPSOM

NONSUCH PARK LODGE *1925* 77072

Beyond the gates, the Ewell Road extends onwards to the centre of Cheam village. This eastern entrance eventually came to be known as Bellgate, since the Bell public house stands further up the hill to the right. The Bellgate Lodge with its leaded windows, battlements and ornamented chimney was demolished in 1938, around the time of the opening of the Nonsuch County School, when this gateway became the rear entrance to the school grounds.

NONSUCH COUNTY SCHOOL FOR GIRLS *1938* 88280

The newly completed school welcomed its first 180 female pupils on 3 May 1938 and was formally opened seven weeks later by the then President of the Board of Education, Earl Stanhope. Under the leadership of its indefatigable headmistress Miss Marion McConnell Dickie MA, the pupils and the nine members of the teaching staff were, within sixteen months, called upon to cope with a variety of unforeseen problems with the start of the Second World War. Miss Dickie retired in 1964, and died in August 1985.

CHEAM PARK HOUSE *1928* 81435

This elegant early 19th-century building was built around 1820 by Mr Archdale Palmer, a London tea merchant, and remained in his family for several generations. It is reputed that Mr Palmer rode on horseback from here to his offices in London every day, taking about an hour for the journey. The house was severely damaged by a V1 flying bomb which fell in these well-kept grounds on 21 July 1944, leaving a crater measuring 8 x 14 feet, and the building was subsequently demolished.

CHEAM PARK HOUSE GARDENS *1928* 81436

The neatly mown lawns and carefully maintained flowerbeds surrounding Cheam Park House are viewed from the vantage point above the porticoed entrance; we are looking down onto the sweeping gravelled drive. The grounds were surrounded by a ha-ha, or sunken fence, which prevented animals from straying onto the property from the surrounding farmland without interrupting the view.

HAYMAKING IN NONSUCH PARK *1925*
77074

This lovely pastoral scene on the Nonsuch Park estate demonstrates that although the internal combustion engine was making rapid progress in the years following the First World War, most farming communities still relied on natural horsepower. This nutrient-rich harvest would provide winter fodder for these hard-working draught animals and others in the months ahead.

IN NONSUCH PARK
1925 77075

Some of these magnificent leafy trees lining, and shading, this lane running alongside the parkland would probably have been mere saplings when Henry VIII and his successor Queen Elizabeth I hunted deer over these grounds. In the foreground, one of these giant specimens has been felled and sawn.

NONSUCH PARK *1904* 51197

Two farm carts make their way down the drive, which is lined on one side with fir trees and on the other with the battlemented brick wall which is generally believed to form part of the original garden boundary of Henry VIII's great palace.

FROM CHEAM TO EWELL AND EPSOM

NONSUCH PARK PALACE *1927*
79473

This is not, of course, the original great Tudor palace of 'None such' built by Henry VIII, which was subsequently given to Lady Castlemaine by Charles II. She, being in debt, pulled the palace down, turned the park into farmland, and sold the contents and materials for building purposes. The land was eventually bought in 1797 by Samuel Farmer, who built this two-storey, castellated house in 1802-05. It stands further east and closer to Cheam village than the original palace. The trees and shrubs in the foreground are growing in the Dell, a turfed-over Tudor chalk pit which may have been dug in the course of the construction of Nonsuch palace.

NONSUCH PARK PALACE *1927* 79471

The asymmetrical frontage of the palace was designed by Sir Jeffry Wyattville, who later went on to work on the reconstruction of Windsor Castle (for which he was knighted), and the Pantheon and St Anne's Church at Kew. The building was further augmented in 1845.

◀ **EWELL,** *The Nonsuch Park Memorial 1925* 76679

Adjacent to the busy London Road and the western entrance to Nonsuch Park, this touching memorial and drinking fountain was erected after her death in December 1906 to commemorate the contribution made by the wife of Captain R C Farmer to the temperance cause. The Farmer family had been in residence at Nonsuch Park Palace for most of the previous century. Although the basin of the drinking fountain and the carved cherub's head are now almost at ground level owing to the elevation of the surrounding area, the inscription praising Mrs Farmer's 'unfailing kindness to all who wanted help or needed sympathy' is still legible. To the right, behind the railings and the stone gateposts, is Redgate Lodge, which was demolished in 1955.

FROM CHEAM TO EWELL AND EPSOM

◀ **NONSUCH PARK**
Palace Entrance c1955 E45034

Here we have a closer view of the impressive entrance to Nonsuch Park Palace, with its stuccoed white walls and the prominent three-storey central tower incorporating angle buttresses, battlements and pinnacles. The kitchen wing of the building belongs to a former 18th-century farmhouse which stood on the site.

▲ **EWELL,** *High Street 1924* 75375

An open-topped double-decker bus rumbles up the High Street on its way to Epsom and Redhill, with the conductor collecting fares from the passengers. Just behind, a cyclist passes the swinging sign of the Green Man public house, which partially obscures the advertising sign for the baker's shop of T G Dunfold.

◀ **EWELL**
High Street c1955
E45028

On the extreme right, the Green Man pub sign advertises its car park facilities, with Dunfold's bakery and Hodges the draper's and outfitter's shop just beyond. On the opposite side of the street, the Lord Nelson pub sports a suspended sign bearing a portrait of the great British naval hero.

FROM CHEAM TO EWELL AND EPSOM

EWELL
High Street 1924 75489

This view, showing the centre of Ewell village, was taken looking north towards the Horse Pond and Spring Corner, and includes several splendid examples of the motor vehicles of the period. A delivery van can be seen at the entrance to Church Street, with the King William the IV pub and its hanging lantern nearer to the camera. On the opposite side of the street a man carrying a suitcase passes in front of the doors of the fire station, next to the tiled butcher and fishmonger's shop run by Mr F Savage.

FRANCIS FRITH'S - AROUND CHEAM

EWELL, *The Old Church Tower 1903* 50512

Three children have been enticed by the photographer into providing a human focal point in the foreground of this picture, with the ivy-clad tower of the old medieval parish church of St Mary the Virgin beyond. The main body of this flint and stone church was demolished in 1848, leaving the tower to serve as a funeral chapel until the start of the 20th century.

EWELL
Bourne Hall c1965
E45079

Formerly Garbrand Hall, this two-storied, five-bayed stuccoed house stands at the centre of the village, and was built on a Tudor site around 1775. The pedimented conservatories on either side of the main building were added later. In 1860 the house was occupied by George and Elizabeth Torr, and by 1879 it was famed for its gardens and its annual display of azaleas, but in the mid 1920s it was turned into a school for girls.

EWELL, *Ewell Castle School c1955* E45003

The largest house in Ewell, opposite the old churchyard, this castellated building was built by Henry Kitchen between 1810 and 1814 to replace an earlier castle which stood here in the reign of King Charles I. Nearby Ox Lane was the site of a skirmish in 1648 during the Civil War. The site of the banqueting hall of Nonsuch Palace lay within the castle grounds until the parkland was divided by the construction of the Ewell by-pass in the mid 1930s. The castle was owned by the Gadesden family until 1901, and subsequently became a boarding and day school for boys.

EWELL
The Horse Pond 1903
50514

The pond is situated at the junction of the London and Chessington Roads. The waters emerging from the springs here are reputed to be the coldest in England, a feature probably much appreciated by the two horses seen in this photograph. On the far side of the pond a smartly-attired coachman in a top hat has diverted from the foot of the High Street to allow his equine companion, and the wheelrims of his trap, to cool in the water. Closer to the camera, an elderly groom restrains another horse. The wall, with a flint and shell archway with Doric columns, allows the waters to emerge from the grounds of Bourne Hall into the pond, before they flow on to the Hogsmill River.

FRANCIS FRITH'S - AROUND CHEAM

▶ **EWELL**
The Spring Hotel and the Coach 1924 75486

The weatherboarded Spring Hotel, in the background at the junction of Chessington Road and Kingston Road, was once a farmhouse, until this stretch of the highway was created in 1834. Previously, the Hogsmill River emerging from the Horse Pond had to be forded by stepping-stones. The Venture coach-and-four, made a number of promotional journeys from London to Brighton, but these passengers arrayed in top hats are probably bound for a race meeting at Epsom.

FROM CHEAM TO EWELL AND EPSOM

◀ **STONELEIGH,** *The Parade c1960* S669057

Stoneleigh took its name from Stone's Farm, at the southern end of Nonsuch Park. Its rapid development followed the opening of the railway station on the Epsom to Waterloo line in 1932. Most of the houses and business premises in this suburb were constructed in this mock-Tudor style in the years leading up to the Second World War.

▼ **STONELEIGH**
The Stoneleigh Hotel c1955 S669038

By 1934, more than two thousand houses had been built within half a mile of Stoneleigh Station, and in March of that year Hanbury & Buxton successfully applied for a provisional licence to build and operate a licensed premises on the site of the old courthouse. This grand building was completed in November of the same year. In mock-Tudor style, with stained glass windows and exquisitely decorated carved barge boards, it was classified as a 'superpub', and incorporated entertainment rooms, a restaurant and a billiard room as well as a large hall for receptions.

FRANCIS FRITH'S - AROUND CHEAM

EWELL
Ruxley Splash 1907
58600

Named after Rokesley, a 15th-century owner of the surrounding farmland, Ruxley Lane links the roads from Ewell to Chessington and to Kingston, and crosses the Hogsmill River south of Tolworth. But in the early decades of the 20th century, this small footbridge and the adjacent, spectacular ford provided the only means of passage across the water at this point.

EPSOM
High Street 1902 48083

Once the village of Ebbisham, its immense popularity as a spa resort after the Restoration, followed by its emergence as a racing centre, brought Epsom to national prominence. This view of the unpaved main crossroads at the junction of the High Street and Waterloo Road gives a clear impression of the original narrowness of the eastern section of the thoroughfare, with the old coaching inn, the Spread Eagle, prominent on the corner of Ashley Road.

▲ **EPSOM,** *High Street 1902* 48082

This view of the western end of the High Street, seen from the forecourt of the Spread Eagle, is dominated by the clock tower built by Butler and Hedge in 1847-48, which commemorates the passing of the Public Health Act in that year. With public lavatories at its base, it replaced an earlier watchtower, and provided a focus for the host of market stalls which occupied the central section of the roadway beyond. On the right is a branch of the London and County Bank, with Dorset's shop next door exhibiting a gleaming display of light fittings. Just beyond, the Commercial Inn advertises its accommodation for cyclists and, in the infancy of the motor car, its good stabling for horses.

▶ *detail from* 48082

FROM CHEAM TO EWELL AND EPSOM

▲ **EPSOM,** *High Street 1924* 75368

This intriguing glimpse into Epsom's busy street life in the years following the First World War is viewed from the corner of Ashley Road and the High Street. In the foreground two ladies, wearing cloche hats, are seated in a small, open-topped saloon car heading towards the Clock Tower; in the opposite direction, a much larger convertible with its boot piled high with suitcases follows a motor-cycle and sidecar towards East Street and Upper High Street. On the left are the premises of the stationer's and printer's owned by E G Pullinger, while on the right, the smart frontage of the Spread Eagle Hotel is framed by flowering shrubs.

◄ *detail from* 75368

The London Evening News vendors' placards stridently announcing 'Mahon: Today's Evidence' reveal that this photograph was taken in the last weeks of July 1924. These proceedings at Lewes Assizes were popularly referred to as 'The Bungalow Murder', and involved the killing of 37-year-old Emily Kaye at an isolated former customs officer's cottage at The Crumbles, a shingle stretch of beach between Eastbourne and Pevensey. She was the mistress of a convicted criminal and womaniser Patrick Mahon, who killed her and then dismembered her body over the Easter weekend that year. The Home Office pathologist Sir Bernard Spilsbury described it as one of the most gruesome cases of his career. Although most of Emily's remains were never found, Mahon was convicted of her murder and executed on 3 September.

EPSOM,
B Division, Woodcote Park 1917 68009

Shortly after the outbreak of the First World War in 1914, the War Office commandeered part of the grounds of Woodcote Park for training purposes and erected a large encampment. By spring of the following year this had become a convalescent hospital for Commonwealth troops, and in August 1916 it was handed over to the Canadian army. The ambulance in the centre of the photograph has the identifying word 'Canada' inscribed on its side.

FROM CHEAM TO EWELL AND EPSOM

◀ **EPSOM**
Woodcote Park 1927 79671

This is the grandest house in Epsom. It was originally built in the 17th century for Richard Evelyn, the brother of the diarist, and remodelled in stone for Lord Baltimore. The Royal Automobile Club acquired the house, along with its 300 acres of parkland, in 1913, when some of the historic interior fittings were dismantled and sold. This majestic and beautifully proportioned building was destroyed by fire on 1 August 1934, with only the balustrade, some stables, the two lodges and a flint boundary wall left standing. It was replaced two years later with a brick façade replacing the original stonework.

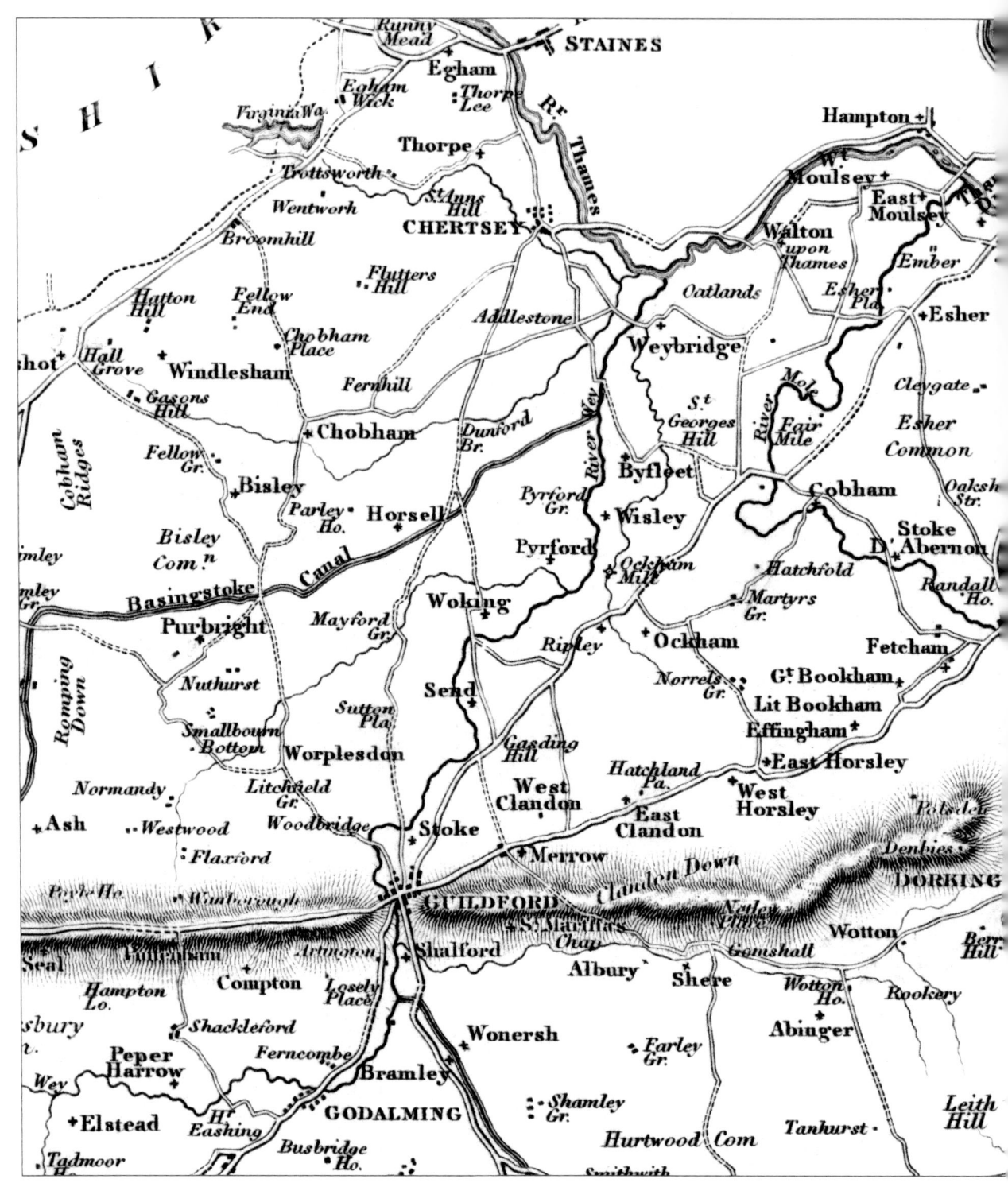

SURREY COUNTY MAP

A SECTION OF A SURREY COUNTY MAP SHOWING CHEAM AND SURROUNDING AREAS c1850

FRANCIS FRITH'S - AROUND CHEAM

CHEAM IN THE FIFTIES

CHEAM, *The Old Cottage c1955* C70061

The old Tudor timber-framed cottage formerly stood slightly further to the south, before being purchased by Epsom Rural Council in 1922 when it was dismantled and transferred to this present site. It had earlier been used as offices by the Cheam Brewery. During the reconstruction process, it was discovered that the timbers had previously been incorporated into an earlier building, leading to speculation that it had once stood in the village of Cuddington before that settlement was demolished by Henry VIII to make way for his Nonsuch Palace.

CHEAM IN THE FIFTIES

CHEAM
Ewell Road c1950
C70007

This relatively tranquil view of the Ewell Road looks towards the cross roads and the foot of the High Street from the forecourt of the imposing showroom and garage of Cheam Motors. Beyond the rebuilt Harrow Inn, the southern side of the High Street is occupied by a large billboard as it awaits its subsequent development, and the roof of the Catholic church is just visible.

CHEAM, *Ewell Road c1955* C70058

On the left, two uniformed schoolboys, probably from either Sutton Grammar or Sutton High School, are about to pass the hedge in front of Cheam Hall as they make their way towards the main junction. On the right, the gleaming curved glass frontage of the Cheam Motors' garage and showroom reflects the passing scene. But the two lines of vehicles waiting for the traffic lights to change on this stretch of the A232 linking Cheam to Sutton and Croydon give a foretaste of the steadily increasing road usage in decades to come.

FRANCIS FRITH'S - AROUND CHEAM

CHEAM IN THE FIFTIES

CHEAM
The Crossways c1950
C70009

This view of Station Road, by now renamed Station Way, shows that while the local branches of W H Smith and Boots the Chemists still occupy their premises below the flats of Cheam Court, the corner shop previously occupied by the branch of Teekoff, whose roasting coffee beans used to scent the air, has been replaced by the estate agency of Parkins & Co, providing a competing service to Soar & Soar on the opposite corner. At the bus stop in Ewell Road, a double-decker on the 408 or 470 route via Sutton to Croydon and Warlingham prepares to take on passengers.

FRANCIS FRITH'S - AROUND CHEAM

▶ **CHEAM**
The Broadway c1950
C70008

In their summer dresses, the ladies of Cheam go about their task of shopping along Cheam Broadway at lunchtime on a warm day. This photograph clearly shows the pleasing symmetry and scale of the sensitive development carried out by the Onyx Property Investment Company at the centre of the village over the preceding decades.

CHEAM IN THE FIFTIES

◄ **CHEAM**
The Broadway c1950
C70006

Ahead, the window display of the branch of United Dairies features pyramids of assorted groceries, while in front two gentlemen take the air seated on a bench which stands above the subterranean cellars of the old brewery. On the eastern side of the Broadway, the sun awnings of all the shops have been unrolled against the summer sun's rays, with, remarkably, the sole exception of the local branch of the International Stores grocery chain. On the extreme right of the photograph the corner site at the foot of High Street awaits its eventual development.

CHEAM
The Broadway c1955 C70053

The shadow of Cheam Court in the foreground indicates that this photograph was taken shortly after noon on this summer's day. The corner site (right), with Price's confectionery and newsagent's shop beneath the flats above, has now been developed. Next to the International Stores, with its sun awning unrolled, is Sergeant's long-established cycle and perambulator shop with advertising signs promoting Raleigh and Rudge products. The spire of St Dunstan's church is clearly visible rising above the shops.

CHEAM, *The Crossways c1955* C70056
The new building on the corner of the High Street, with its three large shops and two floors of flats above, can be seen in greater detail in this photograph. In its substantial size, it is clearly out of scale with the Tudor-styled buildings erected by the Onyx Property Investment Company in the 1930s. This incongruity is matched by the new sodium streetlights mounted on concrete lamp standards that soar above the surrounding roofs. These, I am happy to say, have now been replaced by new lamp standards which are more in keeping with the village atmosphere.

CHEAM IN THE FIFTIES

CHEAM
Park Lane c1955
C70012

This view shows the picturesque weatherboarded cottages that still line the southern side of Park Lane as it curves towards the junction with Malden Road. Behind the partially collapsed brick wall on the right is the garden of Whitehall.

CHEAM, *Park Lane c1955* C70011
Framed beneath the spreading tree, which previously stood within the boundary of Whitehall before the road-widening process was embarked on in the 1930s, is this view of the Broadway looking south. On the right are some of the small businesses, including an ice cream parlour, a radio and electrical shop, a café, and a newsagent's and confectioner's, occupying the old premises at the junction with Park Lane. On the extreme left are the Cheam Parochial Rooms.

CHEAM IN THE FIFTIES

CHEAM
The Library and the War Memorial c1965 C70078

With the spire of St Dunstan's dominating the background, the newly opened public library in Church Road, designed by Masters & Pereira, is visible behind the war memorial. The library stands on the site that was occupied by a field gun when the memorial gardens were opened following the First World War. However, local people resented its inclusion in this setting, particularly when it was identified as a captured German model, and one night local youths removed it and tossed it into the sandpit at Cheam Brickworks.

FRANCIS FRITH'S - AROUND CHEAM

CHEAM IN THE FIFTIES

◄ **CHEAM,** *The Baptist Church c1955* C70010

Whitehall is on the extreme left of this photograph, taken at this junction of Park Lane and The Broadway; the widening of the Malden Road has yet to take place. A female cyclist takes a precautionary glance behind her as she prepares to move out to navigate the reflective sign which indicates the narrowing roadway for traffic heading towards North Cheam. Diagonally opposite is Cheam Baptist Church, constructed on land which was formerly the angle of the garden of West Cheam Manor House.

▼ **CHEAM,** *Sears Park c1955* C70021

Once a cornfield, this open space on the east side of the Sutton bypass was bequeathed in perpetuity to the people of the borough by Mr and Mrs John Sears, who had lived in nearby Quarry Park Rise. In 1934 it was formally opened as a park, and a drinking fountain in Portland stone surmounted by the statue of a young male figure and bearing an inscription acknowledging their generosity was unveiled. By the time this picture was taken, the figure had been removed. Today, only this base with its two carved stone heads remains, and the inscribed plaque is also absent. The small house in the background is currently unoccupied and apparently derelict.

FRANCIS FRITH'S - AROUND CHEAM

CHEAM TO THE SOUTH

CHEAM
The Bridge and Upper Mulgrave Road 1928 81426

We are looking north down the slope to Station Way, and the bridge which dates from the opening of the railway in 1847. Sixty years later the bridge was doubled in width by means of a flat-decked construction in order to cope with the duplication of the tracks. On the right are some of the new detached houses which backed onto the railway at the start of Upper Mulgrave Road.

CHEAM TO THE SOUTH

CHEAM
*Upper Mulgrave Road
c1950* C70004

The parade of shops which lined this section of Upper Mulgrave Road on the approach to the entrance to Cheam Station, which is behind the trees on the left, includes on the extreme right a branch of the Norvic chain of shoe shops, with a local outpost of Sutton Creameries next door. In the distance is the broad concrete bridge installed in 1927-28 carrying the four-lane by-pass south to Belmont and north towards London.

CHEAM, *Upper Mulgrave Road c1950* C70001
We are looking west. On the extreme left is J F White's tobacconist's shop next door to the branch of Lloyds Bank, while across the road is the entrance to Cheam Station Approach, with the offices of Morgan, Baines & Clark's estate agency.

▼ **CHEAM,** *Burdon Lane 1925* 77058

These splendid trees had already overseen the widespread development of substantial suburban houses south of the village and the station which had begun in the years following the First World War. Although by the time this picture was taken the road surface had yet to be tarmacadamed and pavements installed, these luxury properties were eagerly sought after by prosperous middle-class families. It was a trend which was to continue after the Second World War.

► **CHEAM**
The Tennis Courts, Meadowside Road 1925
77070

Situated on the corner of Sandy Lane, these courts, flanked by suburban houses, now form part of Cheam Fields Club. The pavilion in the background, although substantially altered, has also survived to the present day.

CHEAM TO THE SOUTH

◀ **CHEAM**
Banstead Downs Golf Club c1955
C70017

Originally founded for ladies in the autumn of 1890, the club admitted gentlemen to membership within a year, and from a tin hut close to Banstead Railway Station it moved to this site in Burdon Lane nine years later. A putting green was added in 1923, and further major development took place in the years after this photograph was taken.

▶ **BANSTEAD**
The Station c1965 B391114

The station, on the branch line from Sutton to Epsom Downs, opened in 1865, and the white stuccoed house, now a builder's offices, dates from around the same time. The small confectionery kiosk was one of a trio servicing the requirements of commuters, with other branches at Sutton and Epsom. The roof of the station no longer bears the white lettering, and the building is almost a mile from the town centre itself. The road almost immediately makes another sharp bend over the railway line below, before passing the Cuddington Golf Clubhouse and continuing on to East Ewell.

FRANCIS FRITH'S - AROUND CHEAM

BANSTEAD
High Street c1955
B391013

Much of Banstead High Street was rebuilt during the 1920s with a series of shopping parades. The leafless lime tree in the middle distance occupies the spot where the village pond once existed, while All Saints' churchyard is concealed behind the trees on the extreme right.

WOODMANSTERNE, *The Village c1955* W507011
Nestled in the rear slopes of the North Downs, the village derives its ancient name from the Saxon word 'wudmeresthorn', meaning 'thornbush by the boundary of the wood', and was mentioned in the Domesday Book. This 1930s mock-Tudor shopping parade still stands on Rectory Lane as it winds its way south to the junction with the Chipstead Valley Road, where the buildings of the Woodmansterne Treatment Works, belonging to the Sutton and East Surrey Water Company, are just visible.

Index

Banstead
High Street 88
Station 87

Cheam
Banstead Downs Golf Club 87
Baptist Church 82-83
Bridge 84
Broadway 38-39, 43, 76-77, 78
Burdon Lane 86
Cheam Park House 46, 47
Cheam Park House Lodge 33
Cheam School 29
Cheam School Chapel 29
Crossways 74-75, 78
Ewell Road 38-39, 40-41, 42, 73
Haymaking Time 10, 48-49
High Street 30
Library 80-81
Lumley Chapel 37
Malden Road 28
Nonsuch County School for Girls 45
Nonsuch Park 44, 50
Nonsuch Park Lodge 44
Nonsuch Park Palace 51
Old Cottage 38, 72
Park Lane 31, 32, 79
Park Road 32-33
St Dunstan's Church 34-35, 36-37
Sears Park 82-83
Station Way 43
Tennis Courts, Meadowside Road 86
Upper Mulgrave Road 84, 85
War Memorial 80-81
Whitehall 31

Epsom
B Division 68-69
High Street 64-65, 66, 67
Woodcote Park 68-69

Ewell
Bourne Hall 57
Ewell Castle School 57
High Street 12, 53, 54-55
Horse Pond 58-59
Nonsuch Park Memorial 52
Old Church Tower 56
Ruxley Splash 62-63
Spring Hotel and the Coach 60

North Cheam
Gander Inn 25
London Road 20, 22-23, 24
Malden Road 20
The Queen Victoria 20

Stoneleigh
Parade 60-61
Stoneleigh Hotel 61

Sutton
Cheam Road 18, 19
Gander Green Lane 16
High Street 17
Stonecot Hill 24, 25
The Woodstock 24

Woodmansterne
The Village 88

NAMES OF SUBSCRIBERS

The following people have kindly supported this book by subscribing to copies before publication.

As a tribute to P Ashwell
Edward Ashwell, Cheam
The Atkins Family, Sutton - 'For Tom'
Richard Bain
The Barber Family, Cheam
F J Battell
J D Baxter & M D Baxter
Michael Beardmore, Cheam
The Bowles Family, Cheam
Martin Buckley
In loving memory of William Valentine Burden
Bob & Clare Petchley
The Clifford Family
In memory of Mrs M A Cox, Cheam
John & Kathy Dark
John & Kidde Darling, Cheam
To Colin Davenport on your birthday
Paul & Alison Drayton
P E Emery
Christ Church Ewell, Ewell Village
T D Green
P & S Haynes
D Heast
N Mason
The Medcalf Family
Cheryl Morris, a great sister
G Moser & Sons
F Oliver and Family
John Payne
Rachel & Hugh Pearson
George Peterson

Mr P R & Mrs E A Pound
Peter John Rogerson
The Saitch Family, Cheam
The Saunders Family
To the rest of the Scott Family in Macclesfield & Edinburgh
The Shortland Family
Mrs Frances Simmonds
The Sindall Family, Cheam
Angela & Arthur Smith
Frank Station
Tony Stevens
The Tiplin Family, Cheam
Charles Tipper, Aidan J Tipper
Joy & Bill Tresadern
The Wallis Family, Cheam 1935-1984
Mavis Ann White
Graham & Glenda Willis
The Wordsworth Family

Rotary Club of Cheam
50 years 1956-2006

FRITH PRODUCTS & SERVICES

Francis Frith would doubtless be pleased to know that the pioneering publishing venture he started in 1860 still continues today. Over a hundred and forty years later, The Francis Frith Collection continues in the same innovative tradition and is now one of the foremost publishers of vintage photographs in the world. Some of the current activities include:

INTERIOR DECORATION
Today Frith's photographs can be seen framed and as giant wall murals in thousands of pubs, restaurants, hotels, banks, retail stores and other public buildings throughout the country. In every case they enhance the unique local atmosphere of the places they depict and provide reminders of gentler days in an increasingly busy and frenetic world.

PRODUCT PROMOTIONS
Frith products are used by many major companies to promote the sales of their own products or to reinforce their own history and heritage. Frith promotions have been used by Hovis bread, Courage beers, Scots Porage Oats, Colman's mustard, Cadbury's foods, Mellow Birds coffee, Dunhill pipe tobacco, Guinness, and Bulmer's Cider.

GENEALOGY AND FAMILY HISTORY
As the interest in family history and roots grows world-wide, more and more people are turning to Frith's photographs of Great Britain for images of the towns, villages and streets where their ancestors lived; and, of course, photographs of the churches and chapels where their ancestors were christened, married and buried are an essential part of every genealogy tree and family album.

FRITH PRODUCTS
All Frith photographs are available Framed or just as Mounted Prints and unmounted versions. These may be ordered from the address below. Other products available are - Calendars, Jigsaws, Canvas Prints, Mugs, Tea Towels, Tableware and local and prestige books.

THE INTERNET
Over several hundred thousand Frith photographs can be viewed and purchased on the internet through the Frith websites!

For more detailed information on Frith products, look at
www.francisfrith.com

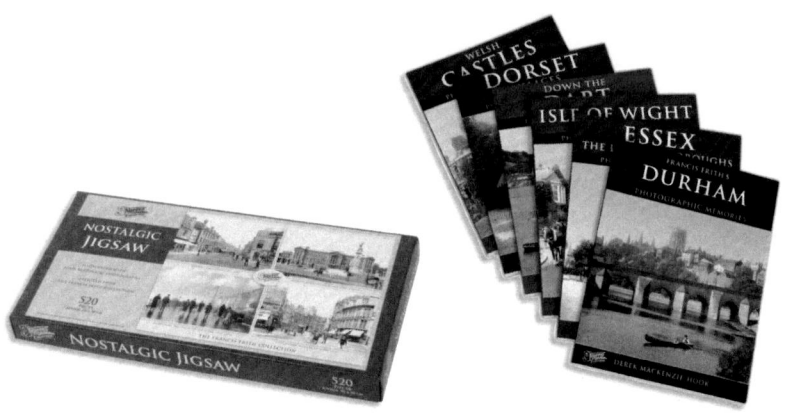
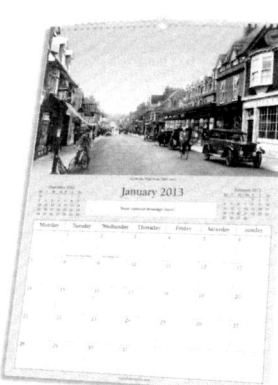

See the complete list of Frith Books at: www.francisfrith.com
This web site is regularly updated with the latest list of publications from The Francis Frith Collection. If you wish to buy books relating to another part of the country that your local bookshop does not stock, you may purchase on-line.

For further information, trade, or author enquiries please contact us at the address below:
The Francis Frith Collection, Unit 19 Kingsmead Business Park, Gillingham, Dorset SP8 5FB.
Tel: +44 (0)1722 716 376   Email: sales@francisfrith.co.uk

See Frith products on the internet at www.francisfrith.com

FREE PRINT OF YOUR CHOICE
CHOOSE A PHOTOGRAPH FROM THIS BOOK
+ POSTAGE

Mounted Print
Overall size 14 x 11 inches (355 x 280mm)

TO RECEIVE YOUR FREE PRINT

Choose any Frith photograph in this book
Simply complete the Voucher opposite and return it with your payment (to cover postage and handling) and we will print the photograph of your choice in SEPIA (size 11 x 8 inches) and supply it in a cream mount ready to frame (overall size 14 x 11 inches).

Order additional Mounted Prints at HALF PRICE - £19.00 each (normally £38.00)
If you would like to order more Frith prints from this book, possibly as gifts for friends and family, you can buy them at half price (with no additional postage costs).

Have your Mounted Prints framed
For an extra £20.00 per print you can have your mounted print(s) framed in an elegant polished wood and gilt moulding, overall size 16 x 13 inches (no additional postage required).

IMPORTANT!

❶ Please note: aerial photographs and photographs with a reference number starting with a "Z" are not Frith photographs and cannot be supplied under this offer.

❷ Offer valid for delivery to one UK address only.

❸ These special prices are only available if you use this form to order. You must use the ORIGINAL VOUCHER on this page (no copies permitted). We can only despatch to one UK address.

❹ This offer cannot be combined with any other offer.

As a customer your name & address will be stored by Frith but not sold or rented to third parties. Your data will be used for the purpose of this promotion only.

Send completed Voucher form to:
**The Francis Frith Collection,
1 Chilmark Estate House, Chilmark,
Salisbury, Wiltshire SP3 5DU**

Voucher
for **FREE** *and Reduced Price Frith Prints*

Please do not photocopy this voucher. Only the original is valid, so please fill it in, cut it out and return it to us with your order.

Picture ref no	Page no	Qty	Mounted @ £19.00	Framed + £20.00	Total Cost £
		1	Free of charge*	£	£
			£19.00	£	£
			£19.00	£	£
			£19.00	£	£
			£19.00	£	£
			£19.00	£	£

Please allow 28 days for delivery.
Offer available to one UK address only.

* Post & handling   £3.80

Total Order Cost   £

Title of this book . . . .

I enclose a cheque/postal order for £ . . . .
made payable to 'Heritage Resource Management Ltd'

OR please debit my Mastercard / Visa / Maestro card, details below

Card Number:

Issue No (Maestro only):   Valid from (Maestro):

Card Security Number: Expires:

Signature:

Name Mr/Mrs/Ms ....

Address ....

....

....

.... Postcode ....

Daytime Tel No ....

Email ....

Valid to 31/12/26

Free Print – see overleaf

Can you help us with information about any of the Frith photographs in this book?

We are gradually compiling an historical record for each of the photographs in the Frith archive. It is always fascinating to find out the names of the people shown in the pictures, as well as insights into the shops, buildings and other features depicted.

If you recognize anyone in the photographs in this book, or if you have information not already included in the author's caption, do let us know. We would love to hear from you, and will try to publish it in future books or articles.

An Invitation from The Francis Frith Collection to Share Your Memories

The 'Share Your Memories' feature of our website allows members of the public to add personal memories relating to the places featured in our photographs, or comment on others already added. Seeing a place from your past can rekindle forgotten or long held memories. Why not visit the website, find photographs of places you know well and add YOUR story for others to read and enjoy? We would love to hear from you!

www.francisfrith.com/memories

Our production team

Frith books are produced by a small dedicated team at offices near Salisbury. Most have worked with the Frith Collection for many years. All have in common one quality: they have a passion for the Frith Collection.

Frith Books and Gifts

We have a wide range of books and gifts available on our website utilising our photographic archive, many of which can be individually personalised.

www.francisfrith.com